BORN TWO

born 2

ALLISON COBB

chax press 2004

Cover photograph: Martin Parr, Magnum Photos

ACKNOWLEDGEMENTS
"The little box book" first appeared as a chapbook edition of *Situation* magazine. Portions of "One-foot a history play" have appeared in *Phoebe, Kenning,* and *Mirage#4 / Period[ical].* "J Poems" and "Polar Bear and Desert Fox" appeared as chapbooks from *BabySelf Press.*

ISBN 0-925904-39-2

Chax Press
101 W. Sixth Street
Tucson, Arizona 85701
USA

Supported by Tucson Pima Arts Council and by the Arizona Commission on the Arts with funding from the State of Arizona and the National Endowment for the Arts.

CONTENTS

THE LITTLE BOX BOOK

Whoever goes to Los Alamos will go crazy.

— Leo Szilard

No father no boy
plunder not
conscious it's
human and not
malicious
immortal its
blooming
roomlets spic

in the box a book
and in that book
another and in
visible waves that
make the fish split
something's un- un-

Then the little box book is more
gone a sort of scorched
awake through all—the fire
storm the indelible
infant crying to itself

the nation's first non-shift Buick
the one-legged soldier
a gift of the President

mom closes necks around hangers
the little b b yawns a crimson
yawn thinks *apple*
tree key and then
saw—the face
she turns it turns wrong

Name this song
Hey Shiny-Cheeked Box
stringing pieces of mouth

Our poison lipsticked little fire top
froths to soothe the rain-
worded—is glue-eyed animal fringe

Here comes Stick walking
his dog along the rim in his
particular hat spinning out of his head

our box—boom
plenty of vanished people
why his eyes are pale

I.
The little box book likes more liquor—grows
back tongues a hydra—children her age blow
candles at blackout birthdays

II.
Strip shops stick like a fungus to rock
potreros ("tongue" in the Red idiom)

Hello is anyone home

III.
And the mountains at night
grow dark stubble grow into a swallow
pretend little box to recall

Little box book song

How now In Re-
covery sweet
cow sweet nut meat sweet
black mouth blew older
brother old brother butcher
to Sunday come
Big One born-in
standing in head up I
thunder go tangled go
leg in your eye

The little box book breaks funny
heels on shaky ankles O
someone is breathing
the mountain blows
ever so kindly she's open
the little box book (and all
that beseems her) game
pieces fluttering . . .
the winner means unbridled fire

Army trucks come
a town sleeping teeth

The sun is scary
the box is a dark-
haired one who would
throw the horny
toad in the road who soils
would cuddle prairie
dogs out of holes who
loved Mother I say
little box in a little

In pea- to marble-sized hail anti-
C-suited workers bump hello NO
HUNTING NO DANGER
box attendants put to masks
free lit cigarettes—the little b b
is strange here we don't know her

To come: an important movie

Novel of the little box book

They ride the train through blackened turf. Melinda bitches with gusto. Nick finds it excites him. He leans toward the rise of flesh inside her shirt and she pushes him back. She loves him but knows it isn't modern, so she punishes, punishes the rotten spot. Pigeons circle the park.

Little box vanish
appear
we're proud
of her care-
ful careful

The box interrupts with its teeth
power and telephone service

a wing
(what is it) a car tire
that quality of lonely—one-foot

John Travolta she says
as a joke another
circle clicks

One of these things is not—
how porcelain the Stick
we have heard that
the hat is like food
on his head
odd the pie recalls
in a jaunty manner
the hot good animal
wolfing down doubt
he can double it
box you are not—Stick
builds the better box
he gives it his throat

Words of the little
box with the little
box inside—what it
grasps in its fists
believes it—this new
one a cry he remembers
to slam
a homeland
he wants a box there
he wants them to burn

The little box book gets out

wanders in from other mornings with strange rubbings a soda
strings No Smoking! signs along the stadium-sized
sawdust pile watches bulldozers doze a beetle
disguise in termite clothes delivers
rat packages in tire grooves stutters
archipelagos T-storm cells plants
flags like water and water-like flags at the mid-
midwater border drives a frig for Babies to Order eyes
the praying mantis in the recycle bin it turned its head visits
the Be Revived room at the Total War store launches
a phone at City Christian produces
personal property for small mammals imitates
the wasp they call tarantula killer reinvents experimental survival

Strong guy the box
can't take its eye off

Snow falls Then ash Then

WHAT have you been watching
Oh little box you've left red prints
all over mother's new Berber baby
blue living—

alright just kidding—here
chew on my hair
the dew is the lumber jeweling

The little box book hangs
upsidedown for feeding
(we close the windows up) poor box
she's nearly half ghost
and her name is nothing

The b b copulates without feeding
proliferates a new anthropology
signs her own moon-
hued Gertrude the speedy
and very detailed—a damsel
fly sipping powdery
moth brains bugling with the elk
the yow of sin season

b b snuffed her
—kiss—piece
tidied out
of her mouth
flew he
to her
Stick she
she nearly
woke up

Stick lectures on the natural box

In case of emergency
contact loose tress
lack translation
it's in itself evidence
mother and offspring
shovel light in the
vacuum mumbling
systematic-like plant

soldier's fingers
stray swollen
conceived into stranger
marks come back
walk of the child
walk of the father
fear beast-bright a box
and then a box

Come watch the little box book form
those bruises will be her eyes

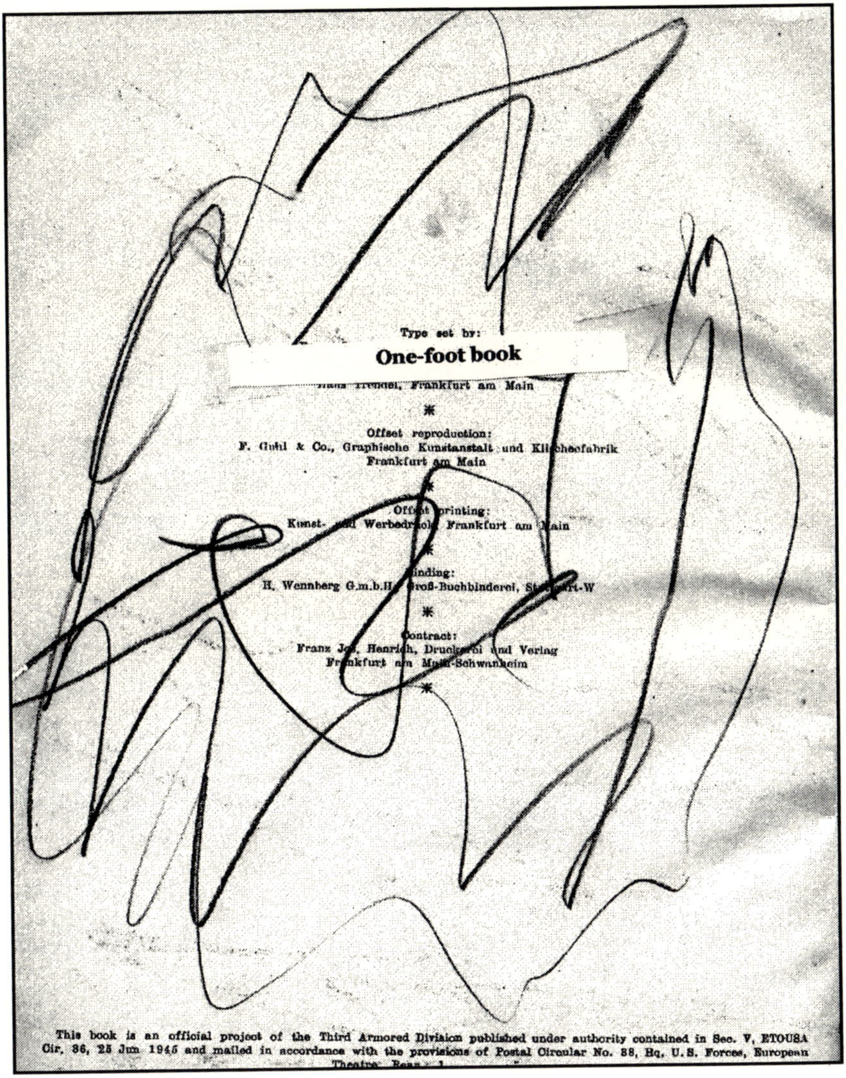

Type set by:
One-foot book
Frankfurt am Main
Offset reproduction:
F. Guhl & Co., Graphische Kunstanstalt und Klischeefabrik
Frankfurt am Main
printing:
Kunst- Werbedr Frankfurt am
inding:
H. Wennberg G.m.b.H. Groß-Buchbinderei, St -W
ontract:
Franz J Henrich, Druck und Verlag
Fr nkfurt am -Schwanheim
This book is an official project of the Third Armored Division published under authority contained in Sec. V, ETOUSA Cir, 36, 25 Jun 1945 and mailed in accordance with the provisions of Postal Circular No. 88, Hq. U.S. Forces, European

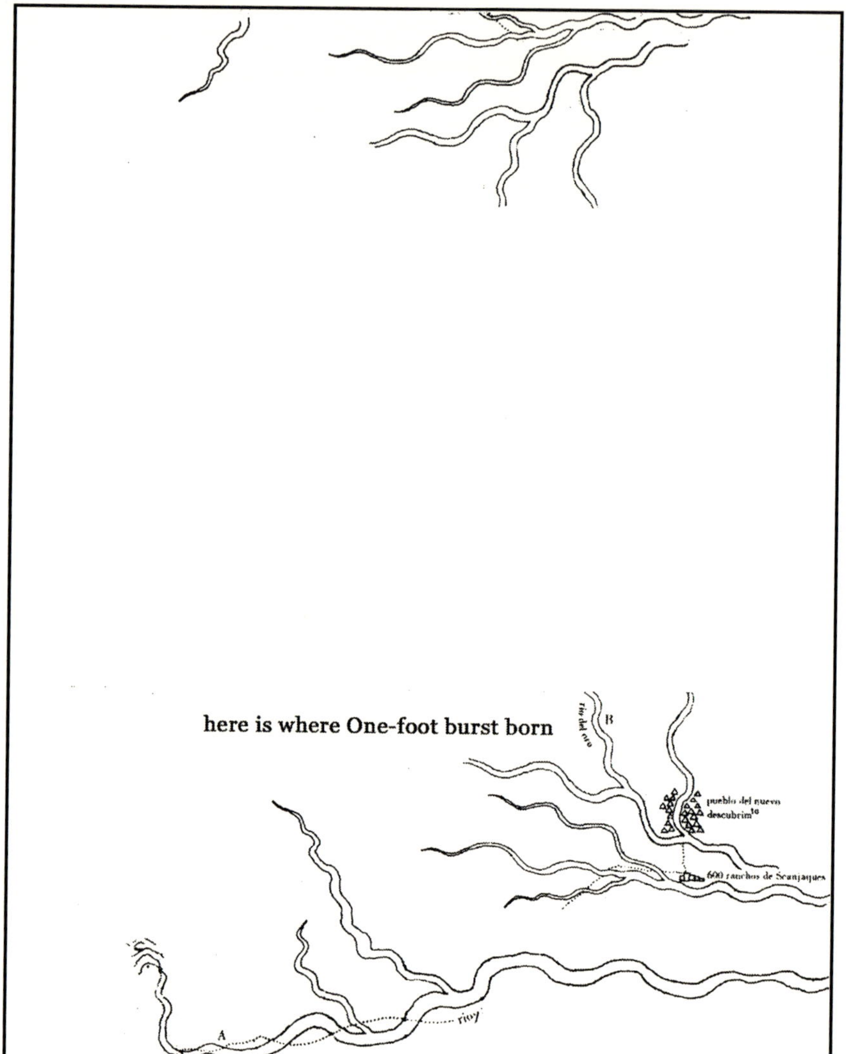
here is where One-foot burst born
rio del oro
B
pueblo del nuevo
descubrim[to]
600 ranchos de Scanjaques
A
rioy

light spilled he

pray rabbit

SO SOLLY!
MOJAVE
DESSERT
rabbit

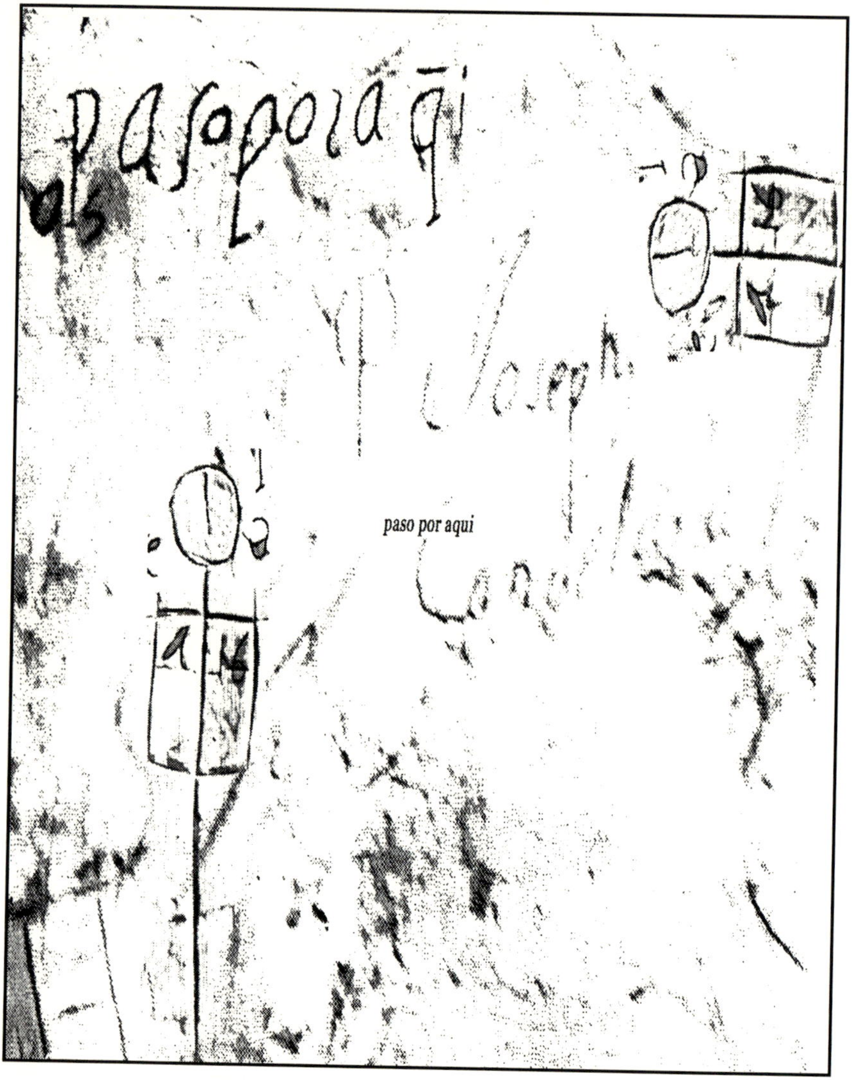
paso por aqui

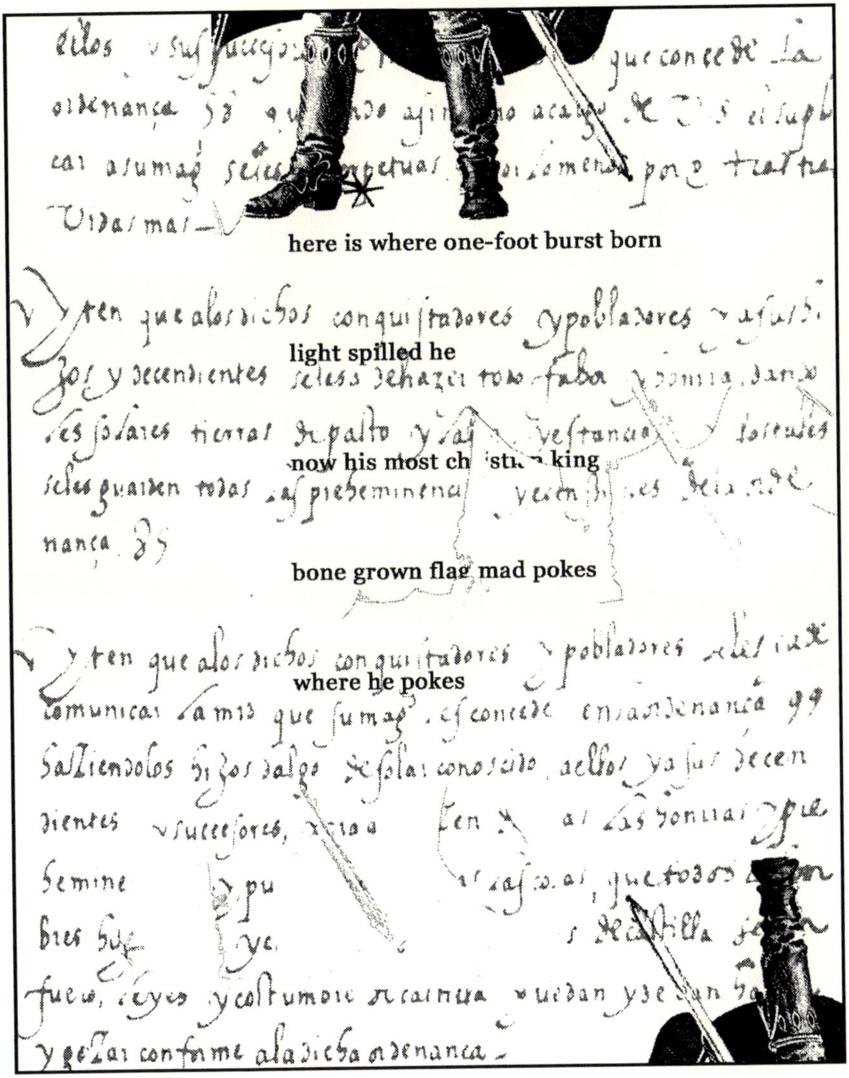

here is where one-foot burst born

light spilled he

now his most ch[illegible] king

bone grown flag mad pokes

where he pokes

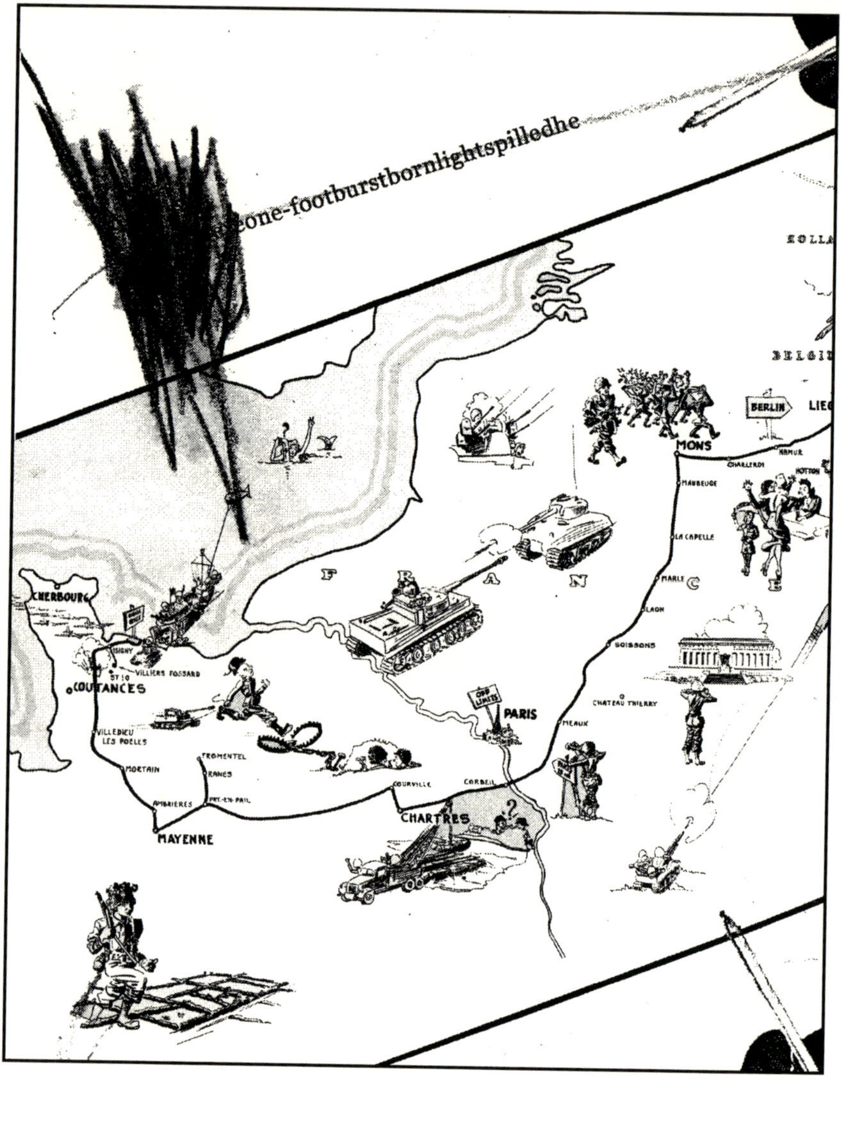
eone-footburstbornlightspilledhe
CHERBOURG
ISIGNY
ST LO
VILLIERS FOSSARD
COUTANCES
VILLEDIEU
LES POELLES
MORTAIN
AMBRIERES
MAYENNE
TROMENTEL
RANES
PRE-EN-PAIL
COURVILLE
CHARTRES
CORBEIL
OFF LIMITS
PARIS
MEAUX
CHATEAU THIERRY
SOISSONS
LAON
MARLE
LA CAPELLE
MAUBEUGE
MONS
CHARLEROI
NAMUR
HOTTON
BERLIN
F R A N C E

membrane.
paso por aqui

ONE FOOT: A HISTORY PLAY

Major General Maurice Rose, 1899-1945

Paso por aqui

— Don Juan de Oñate y Salazar, 1605
Inscription Rock
El Morro, New Mexico

PROLOGUE

This is the story of Rose.
The General Rose was a Major a Rose.

Behold the man with the measuring stick
firm and prompt of decision.

A Rose among dough is a
Rose a spear rising go
dough and boys rising.
How pale it is and how warm is the
dough is the Rose is the thing that is rising.

Rose lived a professional Rose he was
a General who never stayed home. Dirt knows.

ACT I

THE FIRE

People: Here is the fire.

People: This is the fire.

No tourist: This is our house these are our photographs.

People: Here's the old rocker. This is the room where the baby was born.

Feelings: Here is the fire what is it. A fire.

No tourist: This is our house on TV.

Not one: There is that that wants for it all to burn: watching what wants. What wants is many small animals. What wants is exactly thoughts. Dear moss face One-foot we know you what thoughts.

Chorus: The fire is meaningless, the fire has the meaning of moss.

People: The fire is all that means nothing we are.

No tourist: One-foot we are thoughts. We are the moss that thinks what wants and what pains we watch our watching One-foot. Tsk tsk. He is so dramatic.

People: We are the foot are not. This is the fire.

Here is where One-foot bursts
born light spilled he.

You're not born here here here

(Native stolen wife dancing dress
teases One-foot in his teeth. She pees.)

Now his most Christian king bone grown
flag mad pokes gentle faces out.

Where he pokes he
doesn't belong be born.

You're not born here here here
here here

(Don't hear her One-
foot don't hear.)

MOM

Mom, you didn't say anything about the little box book poems. My professor Lorraine Brown noted the mother absence in my bomb work (she was at White Sands, 1950s I think), so I was really proud of the little box book, which is all about you! I'm writing this now about how the Conquistadors came to New Mexico and what happened remains there, like everything else. Some people think One-foot's an Indian, like with the diabetic foot, and it did start out being about grandpa—I didn't even know he was diabetic until we were talking about it at Christmas, or maybe I knew but forgot. But anyway, the one-foot thing because in the war he got his leg blown off and how your grandma lost hers from diabetes and now that *your* father's sick with it and has that sore on his foot. It means characterized by excessive urine did you know that? So anyway first it was going to be about that, but now it is about this. Please let me know what you think.

OVERVIEW FOR FILM PRODUCERS
NEW MEXICO ECONOMIC DEVELOPMENT DEPARTMENT

New Mexico, the fifth largest of the United States, is a land of vast Contrasts: descending from towering 13,000 ft. Mountains, across Mesas, Meadows, Canyons, Arroyos, to stark Desert Expanses, through ancient Native American villages and space-age Scientific Installations. New Mexico is ideally suited to almost any Production requirement.

MOVIES MADE IN NEW MEXICO

1898
Indian Day School, 50 sec., Thomas Alva Edison

1915
Athletic Ambitions
The Auction Sale of Run-Down Ranch
The Brave Deserve the Fair
The Chef at Circle G
The Foreman's Choice
The Girl and the Mail Bag
The Girl, The Villian, and The Dog
Her Slight Mistake
The Tenderfoot's Triumph
Weary Goes A'Wooing

One-foot just wanted to sleep but lacking
a torso as he was he had to be polite—
Greetings cross the weeping
arrow nice to meet you!
One-foot would have liked a crucifixion.
He made it nearly the bones
was so light—all notice—what is it
foot body One-foot.

Before they hollow out the rebel's head the father bends to bless him.

Feelings: Canyons have crotches.

No tourist: In the crotches of canyons lie poisons.

Not one: Of canyons all are justified in their suspicions.

Feelings: One even is known as "Acid"—though that is not quite accurate. Scratch out its fallout face, out peeks another.

People: Names have paws as small animals oh we say they are cute that way we don't speaka your language, moreover you are so much like babies—look tiny fingers!

Small animals: The professor records his reconnaisance of the dead acropolis with romantic thoughts of himself. He knows he had no other choice. This soil has been bad and must be taken prisoner.

Chorus: *So solly!* goes the cartoon bomb America.

Not one: Wet animal mouths at last have found their fresh water—it was earth it was sky it was very low in the ocean.

No tourist: Sound it out until you understand it.

Small animals: One-foot when they found him wore
two blades of grass.

The Rose lost its foot. Someone brained him. Hello broke Rose with one foot is what the guys used to say but not *to* him.

I meant to say lightning fighting the General was major, and smart guys or turnips, which knows more. Oh General O smart guys why are you crying. Save an old pot an old lady. Build a big building. Build it, a biggie. The turnips are singing the rutabagas saying your names are the dead ones with broken eyelids. Sir whiskery sir battering sir Roses: church gap tooth cracks up. What joy it knows at how soft grows your toes.

Pray One-foot says
One-foot. *Fat rabbit come.*
Come rabbit come here.
One-foot puffs he huffs he
tender lets fly his bright
bullet—poof rabbit.
One-foot in this way absolves
each trembly creature.
Saint One-foot.

People: She's got her own orifice
now with a window.

Feelings: Cows have windows for watching stomachs at the agricultural school.

No tourist: Who thinks about cows and makes songs up about them and has cow pictures hung in her room. Who invented a machine
for cow hugging.

Chorus: Eat cow cow
is good for you. One-foot eats cow
when he can get it. One-foot boils
cattle hides for eating. One-foot boils
the boiling he is it.

Small animals: When One-foot came a Conquistador driving herds across the desert he wore a flowered silk suit from China and boots of Italian leather.

People: Warm cows and dusty breathers. Flesh. One-foot eats off his own mouth.

One-foot looks frightened.

One-foot farms fluffs and
slivers looking frightened he
reads a Good book.

One-foot can smell the maiden
water he grows enormous skin chews
his hunger to blood mountains topped
he oozes two rivers.

Do I look pretty he says.

Dear Patrick:

Thank you for your kind attention to my poems. I do agree that they may not yet be fully formed. I'm considering using this excerpt from 1592, which will explain many things:

. . . at twelve noon they recite the Hail Mary, and they sing the alabado at the door of the church, as Your Paternity saw the day you came to visit this pueblo. I have two fiscals, who are very solicitous in this Particular, as is also the governor of the Pueblo, who also helps them, so much so that in ordering the Children to attend prayer services he told them that if they failed to do so he would drive them to mass with Sticks. None are absent, and there I explain to them, through an interpreter, the Mysteries of our Holy Faith and the prayers in accordance with the orders of the Holy Councils, which they Understand very well, as they appear to indicate by the questions they ask me.

I think it is exactly right. Except every time there's a "the" I see "big lizards." Please let me know right away what you think.

1939
The Light That Failed

1941
The Bad Man aka Two-Gun Cupid
Sons Of The Conquistadors
Sundown

X and O. X and O.
One-foot is thinking of war.
Without any arms he thinks to himself
One-foot's feeling a little left out.
One-foot's a dirt city licked by the old rising oceans.
One-foot remembers birds have no arms—One-
foot stick your shoulders out!

Feelings: Hello, I'm looking for the door here.

No tourist: Who has stripped the meat from these fallen animals?

All: Hello again spear and flag and upside-
down soldier.

Not one: Hello again fire.

Small animals: Pointy bearded Conquistadors back from the desert-swallowed bottom of the ocean rattle into the Hotel of Peace in Belgium.

Chorus: *Say! Oh!* say the former doughs, so
hairless and shining.

No tourist: Where the houses are.

Chorus: Where the houses are it knows them from afar.

People: Hello hello fire.

Now Rose has a wound head—how soft it is! Rose has a wound-head and crooked eyeballs, crooked knees goes. *Rest your soft spot here General* some cabbage worms whisper. *Here close your hungry eyeball* say the worms to our pale General. But no, the Rose awakes! He calls the blood to order— *Line up! Line up!* Rose would pry open all folds—Rose, the worms, he knows them, his head is soft and brilliant, it makes small animals jump.

Now Bear sticks his head in—voila!—the bear is all there the bear is all hair and in himself resembles most the missing thing (the limb) the limb all searches have been launched for. Enter Mr. President with his "noodle walk." All the dough boys fall in step. Armless, each tender-headed General has packed up his own hair satchel with teeth. It's the Great Under Earth Ocean Crossing And Adventure—except for the animal gale.

GENERATION 6

No. 54 Karl Ruben Bertil "Bert" Lindeman

Married Ellen Alvida Bolin. Ellen arrived in Rockford when she was 6 years old. She was 12 when her mother died, and two years later her father died, leaving her in charge of the family. She would tell of her trips as a girl to the Nelson Knitting Factory, where she would pick up large sacks of unfinished Socks, throw the sacks over her back, and walk over a train trestle spanning the Rock River to her home. She would sew the foot to the top of the Sock and return them to the Factory.

THE MOVIE

One-foot chases buffalo
hairs devil's breezes blow
over rock nations—oh it is
so suspenseful—beware
the Royal Pleasure flying
arrows—go One-foot he's
anxious for treasure he
kicks up a flock of
blood clots. *Look!*
A miracle! cries
wicked One-foot.

1958
Cowboy
Earth vs. The Spider
Fort Massacre
The Left-Handed Gun

Dear Mr. Wilkstrom:
Enclosed find my $8.00 for the All Occasion Cards by the Mouth and Foot Painting Artists. I would like to request permission to use your pictures in a series of poems I am writing about people who have lost their legs. Your letter states the artists have lost the use of their hands through illness, injury, accident, or birth defect. While my poems deal with people who have lost legs, not the use of their hands, I feel drawn to your project and that it relates in some way to my poems. Please send your reply with my order.

ACT III

One-foot tugs.

Feelings: What is One-foot that tugs
the rotting up mountain up down.

Small animals: The kingdom's bad squirrels he decrees.

Chorus: Is it squirrels he does it is many small
animals.

No tourist: It is what is in its leaping.

People: One-foot grows he
grows flames with his robes.

All: For to punish all leaps he slips
on the wet burns he had longed for—
good One-foot the Good.

One-foot piles up
sheep fluffs beside him he
leadeth them in joyful parley yea.

One-foot would protect
and correct the generations.
He examines considers checks
closely his blinded loin puffs for
signs of betrayal.

One-foot would place
himself at wolf's
mouth *Swallow me! Drink*
my blood! he cries water
pours from his head eyes mouth
arms body and
leg. One-foot his flock he
would save.

1988

Curse II: The Bite

Desperado: Avalanche At Devil's Ridge

Longarm

Made In USA

The Milagro Beanfield War

The Return Of Desperado

The Tracker

Twins

Where The Hell's That Gold?!

Young Guns

Dear Jen: I thought about the limbs, I give them their own personalities living, a kingdom another plane, this seems right to me. What I have left out is how their hands go into the air as if letting their noses know of the rose of their fingers. General Rose was a nose that was never not knowing. The piece I left out about the Conquistador pulsing. I wanted to ask my mother about her mother's mother who came from Sweden and raised her whose leg at the end was cut off, which is why grandma says no one's sawing on grandpa: The loss of the leg may have broken her heart. Who is not a rose and not groves but more like a spear as is Dr. Oppenheimer grinding his bones. Dr. please not so noisy. After all these years we hear it is unpleasant there to remember. Not my father's father whose leg stuck out under the bed at night after the war and he showed us: he put a sock over the stump before he strapped on the wooden part. He didn't seem brokenhearted. I think he even got mistresses (I'm not supposed to say so). How in 1598 one foot was cut off every male resident of Acoma Pueblo by order of the first Conquistador to settle there. This is the part I left out. I had no tape recorder and all the stores in town had closed because of the fire.

Feelings: O footless tree flags on fire, the fire
is a snake is a flag is a fire.
It's a fire it waves.

Chorus: They say burned to the ground aren't they silly.
All burnt down hometowns smell like girl scout
campfires from long ago. Girls, lash a table for
bears and blow the earwigs away, they don't like to eat
off nothing. Sing to them for encouragement and may
your bed be filled with crawling things—what survived
the fire is better a friend, that's our credo.

Small animals: Small animals might have little feet and
that's creepy, but would you prefer a grizzly
or an elk or a deer with their big stupid limbs
they fling out at the least sign of danger?

Chorus: We must marshall the remaining soils
O burping Fathers! O Fathers like fingers
upright in one rough-robed column. Who ever
saw your toes, undisclosed until you've fallen.

No tourist: The mothers are limbless and touch their hats
to the ground in greeting. Slaughtered lambs placed
over the Father's genitals as a warning,
poor little lambs, are arrows to an era
like, more pregnant with meaning.

Not one: The ash of the old neighborhood they say
is dumb and forgiving.

One-foot spies
inside his eye
spider old grannies
distracted touch lambs.
Every little lamb died
with its legs
together. One-foot
tucks this into
his trousers—it
doesn't help One-
foot can hear
can still hear
can still hear
that flap flap.

1990
The Arc
Backtrack
Big Bad John
Over Her Dead Body
Project: Eliminator
Sonny Boy
Sparks: The Price Of Passion
Young Guns II

People: This is the broken dirt thing.

No tourist: And this is the thing of no value that really was vaporized by the fire the leg.

Chorus: In 1.2 seconds she reaches her climax—all it takes is a twitch. All that remains of the suicide lover of the mysterious scientist is a line in a book. That his wife drank too much also is recorded there.

Not one: Who will write a book about it Mr. Rose Mr. "Hop Hop" in charge. The soft snap command could be very surprising to children.

People: The ones who live in pot holes foxholes the "dead" civilization.

Chorus: Dead means not moving.

Small animals: They might be dead they might not be.

Chorus: *After so many it becomes numb to all feeling* she says. *I like to answer questions about the fire.*

CODA

Rose is building the big house of bones. He removes the wifely knick knacks, says hello to himself at the desk.

Greetings General nice to meet you.

One-foot has looked for so long.
Weary goes a'wooing—
Rose the color of amor of war.

Now there are three versions of the story: One-foot a field at dusk in the morning exhaling. One who is left. One whose face turns to lightning spring general forth froth.

This is the dark. It was he who slipped out he who slipped of his very own fingers. Own fellows. Own feels his oars fires. Now our Rose goes.

Limp

limp flags our

Rose eyes to dirt roll.

Greetings nice to meet you.

Dirt eyes grows.

J
poems

CHAP 1

J

hair.

doing

"Get re d

said J

"You look

"What do you mean?"
J
"I just got
these red pants.
I just got
this new shirt.

HAP 4

he

coo

ed

omen

o dance.

She

J

Finally, J

baby,

dance?"

that

her.

thank

baby,"
J
dance."

like
me,"

J
wanted
to dance

"J one dance,"
J

O
J took her hand
to the center
dance

oo
J 's face.
oo happy
she to smile.
"You really did
want to dance with me,

J
really did."

her tight
dance
good.
o
i
she thought.

How would you feel
if someone you didn't know
called you "baby"?

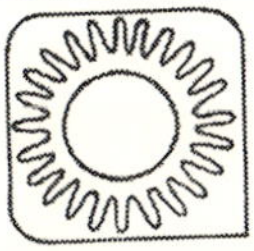

CHAPTER 6

very happy
be J
They

"Hi, J!"
"Hi, J!"
A lot of young women
"Hi, J!"

J knew
so many women.

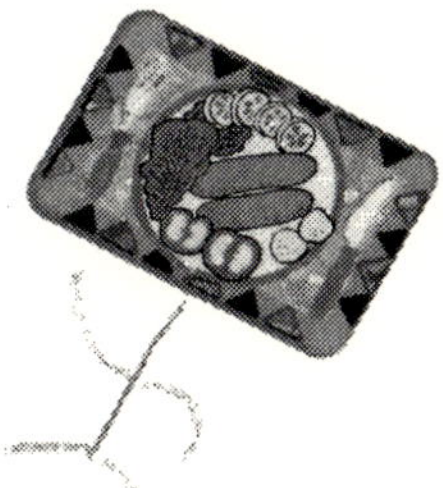

Co-operation of Body

her

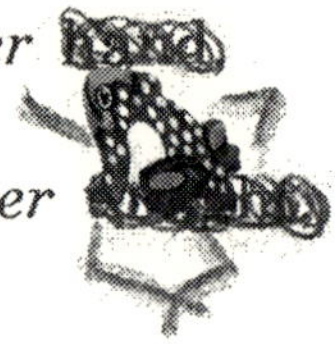

theirs.

her

drink.

Then J said,

you

you

"O

said J

o

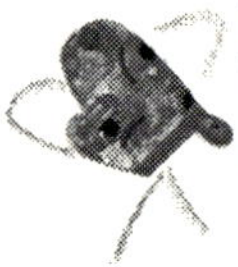

o

ou

"Oh,

I like you.

Come over
and stay just
a little while."

"I like you too, J,"

u u o o

o

"O O"
said J
was
was

she

I
e
t her

The smashing machine (below) squeezes excess air

It

1. Should two
who like
to laugh

2. What is your idea

3. Is going
to do
the first time
two people
Why why

POLAR BEAR AND DESERT FOX

The envious sun kept mum so I asked two copulating beetles: The thirst that from the soul erupts will Bear notice or leave but a kiss in the cup? Her animal drink to me only with thine squid tongues. Exhaust hair my motor and smells I swear we'll wither together. I pledge with mine bed we've carried it outdoors again. Smackover ark blue hands rescues goes dark reach to nubbles for—I can't say it. But thee—J I say here's my back my words and stupid. Dids't only breathe bee stings. Mrs. folds it own ouches. J I say with all and sent'st it. Hope there's a sternum press in our future. Our two sleeps disconnected fingers serious and wiggles. Hello Mrs. Fox she's plugged in grows a rosy outdoors bed. How may I know your divine drink? I ask as all beetles.

If my ear hurts it's red from
Getting real made then who
Has signed in kiss to sparrow
Locks blocked fountains means
Swells in the speculum I and
Thou all atwist spits and glue

Too wide for my thighs my nameless last night kissed her forehead bump. Sleeping no sitting on the toilet to pee what I see of her butt. Blood fling her fingers feel cave times ago those love obligations. THANK YOU ride home from the city so slowing the brood the down blood creep in me. Light I wanted I sick baby sweats watch is this how it is to feel to be. On the back of my life between breathes.

She showed it to me right inside
The embarrassed rolling over so
Doctor J it was into danger
Not sex in that state—this is how we
Like fine things that taste good and are
Quite stupid sparring her art
I show off on to strangers

Today is it fingers her quacks. Me among them. Footless O O my life's sense gone quack quack goes the duck on the roof. Naked among shade turtles arrived my dear picture the rooster. Bear and Fox are gay all day. J am nearly am dead treading fossils. Light among cypress knees where we go we are baby feet that never walked baby spit good for many uses. I have lived this I squished and plucking the legs from. Cool mud fires giant big breathings. I am quack we say quackadoodle Fox and Bear are gay I am sea croissants drunk in the rooster swoop picture my life made while I was all wet away. The duck persist fluffs call the sun up we laugh at it. Love's birdbone bunnies come hunting where Bear and Fox are gay dear gay rooster falls Fox is nearly not here. Morning rolls where it goes babies translucent toes. Dear gay Bear and Fox breathe. Who is nearly not here. Am born over from spit good for many uses. Dear park with feely tarantula. Dear blue rooster.

My life has hundreds of suns ground into her skin in sleep in she frowns in dry cleans. Swallow flap mouth. Fussy poison dress up. Nipplery pants come crowing. I make mouseboy smile in bedland I use my magic hand smells. Bear gets a friend girly wing flair a fruit fly I like don't I circles swamp wink. Spoily underside spiders and mossy. Fox says Fox clean this mess up.

Polar Bear when you
Freeze you disappear
Ears toes what goes
First Fox wonders ginfizzie
Splits in Peru do be
Babies translucent from
Day risen *food!* get it

Fox felt swelling in two of her sleeps in many sleeps the sky broke. When we heard the disaster we were sleepy. When the baseball bat was brought forth having spent the day shopping without we were sleepy. Afterward carrying twins can be a fountain a cause of sleepiness as can loud music. There was the 1950s. Sleepy. Whole centuries have been where one went to work and no one said goodbye because of sleeping beautiful women whose teeth are sleeping and sleep shine for others. I walked with that blanket caught in my throat and the twins I carried inside below water as a different being agreeing with sleep on the tongues of all things and for those without tongues and no faces the sleepiness in lungs that was spreading. Or elsewhere. To be so sleepy just to be saying something. Metal helmeted bat boys searching for the waked up babies are sleeping a kind of sleeping awakeness as in the night Fox's eyes are bright seeing the curve of her Bear in the dark she hears it a bell that is sleeping. Not going to battle not that kind of sleepiness or sleepy nervous having to pee but a sleepy everything touching the smell of a cave is. The smell of her head. Now who is not trying to pretend to be not awake for that is itself sleepy dirt is and all kinds of light I am that sleepy quite Fox thinks.

Mrs. Baby say hips say babushka hair butter. Fresh from bed Bear and Fox do have a motorcycle adventure. Breast press busted bubble cup spiders. Spine yikesy cave head sings sidewalk slaps. Cold where we meet sleeps a cuddle. Flies the mouth very fast smash freckle. Spindle sun cycle jig to the middle two sleeps drying off. Livey life tress thigh arrows vroom blue

Standing it means the monster face restaurant window its lake face the eyes. We can't see so we can't by the sun my life's eyes burned by sleep sex horizon dried the bike between us. When we split we part faces not touching street camera crammed faces the innermost looking not even I see it her looking at her at her looking at her at me

My father's fish finder happy religious people baby what
will I call you her *her*—I am ugly and mean poison-soaked
you are smelly and sweet I am murder you gently expire
your smells in the dark

In the headache cave blood is wood spelled medieval. Do you think you will get back from there. Did one notice the favorite book lacks said female officers. As when days go the millions by shifting the toe itch and then the knee does. Being able to do something "up to it." Polar Bear came Fox's eyes had gone milky. Feeling prior to feeling tuned the "ear" to her this was its "climbing hook." While blinded a show about Noah's ark starring Tony Danza. For the minute years of the woods war my deafening ear tuned to her and the TV my compass directions. The word spiders. I thought they were cousins. We played "war looking." "Noah" in the darkness is a clearing. What swelled and grew into pain everything. My life in me kept one hook.

The many slang words for addict my life
With her paw in the pond I said welcome
Home beer and cigarettes it was she
Who had been gone I said I missed you do
You want it yes she I didn't want to
Go home without it she wants it also yes
she says face twisted up kind of
On purpose cartoon want to ease it

I remember what portion of life is for
Waiting non-times hang
I will say it for you
The house was green
That skin to my insides is unfamiliar
Warm soup to climb
White socks with jeans looks silly
Seams straining she says that quivers
Let's be funny! my mother says to
Be funny that sore looks angry
My violent cells tell
Little Fox tries and tries
Just look at all her muscles

Polar Bear when you sleep you disappear. The American in Colombia she likes the war. Some mothers march after the sons of their fingers. My crotch companion with inner lip longer. Mirror hides a secret message code kit. In the valley of nipples I said *flowery* in September (laugh from audience). In December say *wing* say no *flap*. I say in her rugged chambers. Mirror works up a huge blind spot. We squirt. My life came with cigarettes those for swims and dynamite sticks. Feelings of low self-recognizance. A hair peculiar two females what are. Fox and Bear go up up down kiss. J's hair reels in not a fish what we want it's a big one. Woven of the red sand deserts are dry things Australia and flying. Polar Bear I can make you back with the lamps in my fingers. My fingers in the mother her nipples. Straight line means girl baby. This is a girl says the monitor. I want to know. So I look.

Polar Bear and Desert Fox decide what to do
Babies like to look at each other
You're face looks sleepy because
It's sleepy look out of it!
What what what thinks
Fox she knows what but she can't
She pink as what smarts

Exciting to remember. As it is exciting to remember a sex scene. As it is to be remembering watching being. A woman not to be remember. As a woman the being. Even though the being is murdered it is still exciting the sex scene. As the being is by her enemies the two woman beings. This is as they say documentary. In the sex scene and Fox imagines cameras in the building. Watching as being that form which is not man not humping. That humping as joy that kind of pounding demanding laughing. How that movie mainly unrolls into eyes Bear and Fox's small pockets being. Of existing how little these see the two woman as this form being. And what happens. How to imagine it howly. Humping we like and are laughing. Between two the giant not seeing. Of fishing tossing it again. We laughing feeling afraid as we are.

Bear is sick. Fox fears faces at looking for that kind of poor. Bear is Fox's fault for her sick my life's cough. Turned down in her the unspeakable. Dream she puts her finger in the butt THWUCK hilarious cartoon selves and nibbles. The bride that fell on the poodle. Har har Foxes fall sweats fly. As if but our world would be feat and private interior. O Fox's baby bone girl. That it comes from inside her far distances. Sweaty little baton twirlers. She fashions a tuna belt buckle with felt can I call her. Smelling itself as Friday dirt curbs. Two spines of course it is woman with cave a small child and orange. Two brave girls.

Polar Bear did disappear. Dirt eye. She and her. She and her Desert Fox have scratched out a Lenten calendar. For each day one body part twice titled butt butt for example. Goes Fox. Her face is and they're unfurling through their kiss calendar. Sparkly cars fly to be beautiful breaking each floosh of glass and metal. Nice men in gyms turning pedals strain quite kindly to remember. Niagara Falls dress in my face bones of monsters and inside the bones the idea of monsters quite porcelain and sentimental. Mr. Fugitive with his captive—two brightnesses. That woman the baby came from she clung with it to the tree. That glow is her face a boy born and raised in a rowboat. A baby and something different. J I thought once—a cup and erect. Look my love we make all that trembles and all. That trembles the names from us.

ABOUT THE AUTHOR

Allison Cobb was born in Los Alamos, New Mexico, and now lives in Brooklyn, New York. She is the co-editor of POM2 literary magazine, an editor of *BabySelf Press* and the author of numerous chapbooks. This is her first book.

OTHER BOOKS published by CHAX PRESS

Elizabeth Treadwell, *Chantry*
Beverly Dahlen, *A-Reading Spicer & 18 Sonnets* (New West Classics 3)
Jonathan Brannen, *Deaccessioned Landscapes*
Todd Baron, *TV Eye*
Karen Mac Cormack, *Implexures*
Pierre Bettencourt, *Fables*
Heather Thomas, *Resurrection Papers*
Nathaniel Mackey, *Four for Glenn*
Charles Bernstein, *Let's Just Say*
Hank Lazer, *Deathwatch for My Father*
Robert Creeley, *Yesterdays*
Keith Wilson, *Transcendental Studies* (New West Classics 4)
David Bromige, *As in T As in Tether* (New West Classics 2)
Mark Weiss, *Figures: 32 Poems*
Benjamin Hollander, *Levinas and the Police*
Gil Ott, *Traffic*
Kristen Gallagher, ed., *The Form of Our Uncertainty: A Tribute to Gil Ott*
Diane Glancy, *Coyote's Quodlibet*
Lyn Hejinian & Ray DiPalma, *Chartings*
Nathaniel Tarn, *The Architextures* (New West Classics 1)
Hugh Steinberg, *In the Attic of the House of the Dead*
Beth Baruch Joselow, *Self Regard*
Diane Glancy, *Closets of Heaven*
Diane Glancy, *(Ado)ration*
Camille Martin, *Magnus Loop*
Peter Ganick, < *a ' s a t t v* >
Lisa Cooper, *& Calling It Home*
Phillip Foss, *Chromatic Defacement*
Diane Glancy, *A Primer of the Obsolete*
Lydia Davis, *Blind Date*
Lisa Cooper, *Tilt Rail*
Rae Armantrout, *writing the plot about sets*
Tenney Nathanson, *One Block Over*

Tom Raworth, *Three Poems*
& Charles Alexander, *Pushing Water part 7* (in one volume)
Karen Mac Cormack, *The Tongue Moves Talk*
Bob Perelman, *The Masque of Rhyme*
Eli Goldblatt, *Speech Acts*
Hank Lazer, *3 of 10*
Tom Mandel, *Prospect of Release*
Myung Mi Kim, *The Bounty*
Mary Margaret Sloan, *The Said Lands, Islands, and Premises*
Kathleen Fraser, *when new time folds up*
Norman Fischer, *Precisely the Point Being Made*
Nathaniel Tarn, *Caja del Rio*
Rosmarie Waldrop, *Fan Poem for Deshika*
Lisa Cooper, *The Ballad in Memory*
Nathaniel Mackey, *Outlantish*
Eli Goldblatt, *Sessions 1-62*
Ron Silliman, *Demo to Ink*
Beverly Dahlen, *A Reading 8–10*
Gil Ott, *Wheel*
Karen Mac Cormack, *Quirks & Quillets*
Susan Bee & Charles Bernstein, *Fool's Gold*
Sheila Murphy, *Teth*
bp Nichol, *Art Facts: A book of Contexts*
Charles Bernstein, *Four Poems*
Larry Evers & Felipe S. Molina, *Wo'i Bwikam / Coyote Songs*
Mei-mei Berssenbrugge, *Mizu*
Charles Alexander, *Hopeful Buildings*
Lyn Hejinian & Kit Robinson, *Individuals*
Eli Goldblatt, *Sessions*
John Randolph Hall, *Zootaxy*
Paul Metcalf, *Firebird*
Karl Young, *Five Kwaidan in Sleeve Pages*
Anne Kingsbury, *Journal Entries*
Charles Alexander, *Two Songs*
Paul Metcalf, *Golden Delicious*
Jackson Mac Low, *French Sonnets*